Choices:

Death, Life and Migration

Choices:

Death, Life and Migration

Dr. Patricia Rumer

Pat Rumer

Printed by CreateSpace

2018

The events and conversations in this book have been set down to the best of the author's ability, although some names and details have been changed to protect the privacy of individuals.

Patricia Rumer
pjrvocera@gmail.com

First paperback edition December 2018

Photograph on page 13 by Joene Pike
Photograph on page 29 by Marjorie King
Photograph on page 51 by Randall Shea
Book design and graphics by Mark Slatin

ISBN 978-1729661048

www.justiceactivist.com

Dedication

This book is dedicated to the courageous men, women and children who risk their lives to journey to the United States and the resilient people in Guatemala who have never stopped working for justice.

All royalties from the sale of this book will go to two immigrant rights organizations: The Interfaith Movement for Immigrant Justice in Oregon and the American Friends Service Committee's U.S.-based immigrant rights programs.

Table of Contents

Preface

The stories in *Choices: Death, Life and Migration* emerge from almost fifty years of my living two lives — one in Guatemala and the other in the United States. When I first went to Guatemala in 1969 as a young North American volunteer with the American Friends Service Committee, I lived in a small indigenous village in the northern highlands. At that time there was only one person in the village with a relative in the United States. By 2010, about one-half of the village had a family member living up North. Such is the way of migration.

In the spring of 2012, I joined Los Porteños, a Latinx writing group in Portland, Oregon. I wanted to write with people who shared a passion for the culture and history of Latin America. Los Porteños has challenged and inspired me to remember and to write about my double life and, especially, to share the stories of the strong and resilient people I've met in Central America and in the United States.

In the summer of 2014 I had just returned from three months in Guatemala, where I had been working on a memoir of my justice journey, which began many years earlier in Guatemala. From conversations with Guatemalan friends and from reading local newspapers, I knew of the sharp rise in drug violence and violence against women. Unemployment rates, especially among young adults, were high and 85 percent of the indigenous population was living in extreme poverty. When the first group of Central American youth entered the United States seeking safety from these conditions, I was not surprised.

What did surprise and shock me was the Obama administration's reaction. The government either detained the youth in large, concrete detention centers in Texas or instantly deported them back to the dangers of the country they had just fled. I was angry and frustrated. I wanted to do something.

Several months later, in the winter of 2015, I set the larger book project aside to focus on justice work at the border. However, one of my writing mentors said recently, "Pat, you owe us [this] book. Tell us your stories of the Central American people who have enriched and changed your life."

These stories are real; only the names of immigrants have been changed for their protection, as for them it is a matter of life and death. Such decisions are part of every story in this book.

As a North American, middle-class white woman, I have had the privilege of traveling on a U.S. passport. I have many identities: social justice activist, blogger, journalist, human rights observer, immigrant accompanier, teacher and friend. These identities are the lens and I am the *vocera*, giving my voice to the voices of the strong people who make the difficult decisions to migrate north or to stay and struggle for better lives in Central America. Whether migrating or remaining, people face hard, life-threatening challenges.

Immigrants are just like you and me. They want to live, raise their children in a safe environment and provide them with educational opportunities leading to a better life. Since these dreams are not possible to achieve in many parts of Central America, many people migrate north hoping to reunite with family already in the United States. Despite this time of painful, disruptive and inhumane U.S. immigration policies, their stories can offer hope as to how we can "welcome the stranger."

Acknowledgments

Thanks to Los Porteños for their friendship, support and creative opportunities where several of these stories were shared. The poems *Who Is "He"?* and *¿Quién es "él"?* were published in the March/April 2014 *Tribuno del Pueblo*, a bilingual newspaper in Chicago, Illinois.

I am grateful to my writing mentors and teachers: Esther Elizabeth Armstrong, Jen Violi, Lawson Fusao Inada, Martha Gies and Kim Stafford as well as the other workshop participants.

Thanks to my editor, Carolyn Lane.

Special thanks to my project assistant, Mark Slatin, who conducted research, created the graphics and designed the layout. His work has enhanced the quality of this book.

Deep gratitude to my sister, Connie Rumer, and my daughter, Deborah Sposito. They have read my stories, given loving critiques and always encouraged me to share my memories.

Thanks to Joene Pike for the photo of Manuel and Carlos on page 13, Marjorie King for the picture in the Casa Alitas kitchen on page 29 and Randall Shea for the picture of the *básico* students on page 51. All other photos were taken by me.

Introduction

Choices: Death, Life and Migration is a collection of stories written over several years, all gathered from my Guatemalan experiences within that culture. In the first set, I wanted to show parts of the culture that few people see or know about, including the choices that people are forced to make. Each of these stories relates to a time and place and people I encountered as I moved into and about Central America, beginning in 1969 and continuing to this day.

Death Is for the Living: *Día de los Muertos* is comprised of poems and stories about Guatemala presented at the annual *Día de los Muertos* events sponsored by Los Porteños in Portland, Oregon.

- *Death and Zopilotes* came from a visit to the cemetery in Guatemala City during a study leave researching a larger book on my forty-five-year involvement in Guatemala.

- *A Guatemalan Wake* reflects many experiences and occasions of learning during my two-year stay in Guatemala working in community development with my husband Carlo.

- *La Tierra Sagrada* was written after I visited Santa María Tzejá, Ixcan, Guatemala, as a member of a sister city church delegation.

- The poems *Who Is "He"?* and *¿Quién es "él"?* emerged from a Guatemalan Human Rights Commission/USA delegation to the Ixil region of Guatemala to hear first-hand from the survivors of the armed conflict.

The second set, <u>Migration or Immigration?</u>: *Migrar no es delito,* is about the burning issue of immigration. There are stories of Central American immigrants that I worked with in Arizona. Another story in this section offers a Guatemalan perspective on migration, while the final piece asks what can we in the United States do about it.

- *¡Bienvenida!* reflects the stories I heard from women in the Casa Alitas shelter and Casa Mariposa Detention Center Visitation Project, Tucson, Arizona.

- *Acompañamiento* concerns a woman whom I befriended in the Eloy Detention Center, Arizona, until her release.

- *Becoming an UndocuAngel* explores ways that U.S. citizens can support undocumented immigrants.

- *Crossing Borders* resulted from a return trip to Santa María Tzejá, as a member of the sister city church delegation, to learn how Guatemalans viewed migration.

- *Accompaniment Continues* is a call to get involved with some specific recommendations based on my own immigrant accompaniment experience.

Día de los Muertos

Death Is for the Living

Death and *Zopilotes*

The Garbage Dump and a Cemetery

Guatemala City, Guatemala — 2014

While the woman stands across from the ravine, swirls of black vultures circle and swoop. There is a wake of these *zopilotes* hovering over the ravine where the dump is located. They are here for food while she is here to bear witness in a human rights delegation. They soar and dive straight into the dump looking for something to eat or to nibble on.

On one side of the dump is the cemetery, full of dead people in little houses. She can see the gap between wealthy and poor in death as in life. The wealthy build elaborate homes to house the deceased. The poor buy a box or shelf in a mausoleum — flowers are hanging out of the shelves looking like a brightly decorated apartment house. A friend explains the system to her: the poor, if they don't have the money, rent the space and pay monthly. If they miss a payment, the remains are removed and buried in a common grave. They make a choice between the grave site and rent and food. Even after death, there is a pay-as-you-go plan.

How can you honor your dead on *Día de los Muertos* if their remains have disappeared? Do people still visit the mausoleum shelf and imagine that their loved one is there? How can they remember their loved ones at this cemetery overlooking the garbage dump with *zopilotes* circling around like shadows of death?

At the edge of the cemetery is a deep ravine. It is a beehive of activity — big yellow trucks line up to dump their refuse; people follow the trucks to see if there is anything of value inside and they raise their hand to indicate, "This is my truck." From high on the hill, the garbage pickers look small in contrast to the huge mounds of garbage. Some carry big bags of recycled trash that they have reclaimed and others are still sorting through the garbage — the line of trucks is endless. It smells like rotten garbage and she imagines the smell of rotting bodies. A bandanna tied around the woman's face covers her nose. The refuse is dumped and the vultures swoop and dive. She sees a group of vultures on a nearby hill — they look like gnomes bent over talking to each other.

This is the other end of consumerism — the plastic bottles, paper bags and boxes, old mattresses and furniture — the death of things, not people. The garbage that she tosses in her hotel room ends up here. If she does not consume, then there is no trash or, maybe, less of it?

The garbage pickers are entrepreneurs. They know the price of all the trash in a market economy. Some of them specialize in jewelry and some, the divers, literally dive into heaps of refuse to look for more valuable things. She sees men and women with bandannas tied around their faces and plastic bags covering their feet. Hands search for valuables in the refuse. One man found a huge diamond once. Since then the number of jewelry divers has increased.

She is sobered by what she has seen — the smells, the dying gardens in the mausoleum, the rotting flesh and foodstuffs, and the excess that people throw out for other people to rescue. There is the cemetery on the hill overlooking the garbage dump in a huge ravine — death in many forms.

The *zopilotes* are happy, as there is an abundance of rot for them to scavenge. It is a macabre scene, but as she imagines the families on *Día de los Muertos* — bringing food and blankets, eating, singing, drinking and even dancing among the little houses — she sees how full of life it is. When the families leave, the *zopilotes* will have a feast of their own.

A Guatemalan Wake

San Francisco La Unión, Guatemala — 1970

I nudge my husband, Carlo. "Someone's pounding on the door. You go, I'm cozy in bed. It's too damn early!"

"Don Carlo, Don Carlo." The pounding continues.

"Ok, I'm coming." He throws open the door. "*¿Qué quieres?*" A small boy about ten years old is trembling with fright or the cold in the doorway. "Don Carlo, come quick, my father has fallen from a tree and he can't speak."

"Ok, José, let me get dressed. Pat, you need to get up too."

Grumbling, I slowly stretch and wake up. It's still the rainy season so it is damp and cold in the early morning. I shiver as I pull on long johns, a warm sweater and jeans before I go outside.

Pedro's son, José, is standing patiently outside our front door. "José, why are you here?"

"Doña Paty, my mother said that you would know what to do."

My heart stops. I don't have any idea what to do.

Carlo turns to me, "Stop the next bus down to Xela and ask the driver to get a message to Madre María that she's needed!" There is no doctor in this small village. Madre María runs our local health clinic and people trust her.

When they leave, I have a heavy heart. What if he's dead? What will happen to his family? I murmur a little prayer that Pedro will be okay.

Several hours later, Carlo returns with a downcast face. "He had a bad heart. The fall affected his heart and he died instantly."

I hug Carlo and we hold each other silently. José's father was so young and he had four kids. José is the oldest. After seeing Pedro's body, Madre María tells the family that they must prepare the body for burial as soon as possible. Even though it's cold at night in the *altiplano* (highlands) there is no refrigeration to keep the body cold.

"But Madre María, we must have a wake for him. Our family, we want to say goodbye to him and invite his friends to remember him," Pedro's cousin Juan says.

María nods her head. "All the sisters will attend the wake to show respect to Pedro and his family."

"Pat, we have to attend the wake!" My heart beats rapidly. "I don't know, Carlo, I've never seen a dead body."

"What, how is that possible?"

"Look, I was raised Presbyterian — we don't do funerals, only memorial services to remember the essence of the person. No bodies! Now, I'm in Guatemala and you expect me at age twenty-nine to attend a wake and to be comfortable with a real, dead body!" I feel sick to my stomach.

The next day we walk up a narrow path with steep sides to a small mud house perched precariously on the side of a hill. It is misty and cold. I hold onto Carlo's hand for balance and complain that my feet are cold. As we approach Pedro's house, we can hear singing and wailing.

A family member opens the door, "*Pase adelante.*" He motions us inside.

I don't know what to expect. I blink in the almost-dark house. There is one naked light bulb dangling from the ceiling directly over the body. Pedro is on a plank in the middle of his small, dirt-floor house. He is wearing work clothes but no shoes and looks as if he's sleeping.

We greet his wife, Doña Filomena.

"*Lo siento mucho,*" we add our condolences. She is weeping with her face almost covered by her shawl. She nods her head as she doesn't speak Spanish.

The men are drinking *cusha*, the local moonshine. They offer Carlo and me a drink — it tastes like turpentine and burns my mouth. After one small swallow, I politely decline a second sip.

Everyone is busy doing something, but I'm neither a relative nor a local. We are invited guests. I smell beans and chicken cooking in big pots suspended over an open fire on the floor. Smoke curls up and out the one window in the house. I begin to cough from the smoke and move quickly away from the fire. I bump into the plank. *Oh no! Now I've done it!* But luckily no one seems to notice.

Two women kneeling are making *tamalitos*. Carlo and I are taller than most of the community so we really stick out. I move over to stand by the wall and shrink into it. I begin to breathe heavily and feel claustrophobic; I look anywhere but at the dead body.

Why is Carlo so much at home? He is comfortable and I am not. I am thankful for his presence and appreciate the ease with which he greets people.

Pedro and the plank are surrounded by women cooking, men drinking, children running around with a few chickens wandering in and out. Women are breastfeeding their babies. Then, food is passed to us in small bowls — chicken stew with *tamalitos*. We did not know to bring our own plates so Pedro's family has shared theirs.

The simple act of sharing food relaxes me. As I look around the room and see the families caring for each other, I begin to feel better. I realize that in the midst of death, there is so much life. The wake is messy — with loud wailing and boisterous singing — but it is vibrant and alive. After several hours, we say our goodbyes and leave. We want to get down the rutted path before night falls.

La Tierra Sagrada

Sacred Earth

Santa María Tzejá, Guatemala — 2003

It is another hot, humid day in the Ixcán — a remote area in Northern Guatemala. Manuel guides members of the church delegation silently through the jungle to the killing fields in his *pueblo*, Santa María Tzejá. When we reach the place of the 1982 massacre, Manuel's eyes fill with tears.

Softly, he tells his story. "I was working on my parcel of land some distance from the village. My infant son was crying and my wife asked me to return to the village for milk and food. My six-year-old son, Carlos, and I went quickly down the path to the village. On our return, we heard gunfire and ran towards our *parcela* (farming plot). Then, only silence and the pitiful cries of the baby."

Manuel falters in telling this story of the brutal slaying of his wife, four children, mother and two cousins.

"Why were they killed?" he asks.

We are humbled by this simple, direct question about a tragic period in Guatemala's long history of violence and death. Who knows why Manuel's family was killed? Certainly, it was part of Ríos Montt's scorched earth policy to root out the guerrillas and protect the civilians. This policy, named *fusiles y frijoles* or "rifles and beans," meant that these villagers had to make a choice — either for the government or against it. If villagers joined the government campaign against their people, they were given beans; if they opposed the government and the military, even passively, they were shot by rifles and killed.

Manuel did not know why their village was singled out — was it because of their progressive priest, Father Luis, or the trained catechists who had studied the Bible from a liberating perspective or the fact that their cooperative had capable leaders? The scorched earth policy targeted catechists, teachers, agricultural cooperative leaders, health workers — in fact, anyone who could and did educate and organize the community.

"War is not the answer," Manuel tells us. "The Guatemalan civil war brought us only *dolor, pobreza y miseria* (sadness, poverty and misery) — people think that nothing will happen in a war, but that is not true." Manuel fled Guatemala for Mexico, where he and his new family lived until their return in 1994.

12

We stand in this sacred place. Tears fall from our eyes as we mourn the terrible losses Manuel, his family and so many other Guatemalans have suffered. Manuel speaks with hope about a legal case against General Ríos Montt that he and other returnees have filed with help from the Center for Human Rights Legal Action.

I am overwhelmed because I am connected to this man's story. I think back and remember how my journey with the Guatemalan people began in 1969 in San Francisco La Unión, a small village in the *altiplano*. Manuel and the other villagers are K'iche'-speaking, indigenous Guatemalans, originally from the highlands, who moved to the Ixcán in the early 1970's.

In the highlands, the majority of indigenous people struggled to survive — the poor soil and lack of good farmland meant one had to work very hard to produce enough corn on these little *parcelas* — and the resulting poor diet made things difficult for their families. They traveled a long distance to find land in the Ixcán with Father Luis Gurriarán.

The villagers from Santa María Tzejá formed an agricultural cooperative — built simple homes, a church and a school. They had heard that there were armed battles in the area between guerrilla forces and the military, but they were not part of either struggle. They just wanted to farm their land, feed their families and, hopefully, educate their children.

Back in the present and we've arrived in Santa María Tzejá in time for the twenty-first anniversary of the 1982 massacre. Father Luis Gurriarán had worked with Father Bill Woods, a priest who died in a mysterious plane crash in 1976. Father Bill, like Father Luis, had bought land in the Ixcán to found agricultural cooperatives. I had considered working with Father Bill back in 1969 when the resettlement of landless *campesinos* (farmers) began in the Ixcán area.

During the intervening years, my life and work had taken me frequently to Guatemala, working on development projects and accompanying refugees on their return from Mexico to the Ixcán.

Father Luis says, "Pat, you are a *veterana* — a person who has been part of our history." I feel at home in the villages of Guatemala — thinking, dreaming and speaking in Spanish.

Ten years later, in May 2013, a Guatemalan court found Ríos Montt guilty of genocide and crimes against humanity. However, that legal decision was annulled within two weeks. I heard the news on the radio and was devastated. The initial decision had left me feeling hopeful that some measure of justice would be done. Overturning the judgment against Ríos Montt felt cruel in the face of all he had done to the Guatemalan people.

14

In 2013 Manuel wrote, "Our war experience has shown us that many families suffered massacres, but in almost every case, there was a survivor. And here with us, Edwin got out alive; he escaped from death. Even back in 1982, I believed he would be called to do something special in his future. He is now involved in this genocide case."

Another survivor, Edwin Canil, is a witness to the massacre and a lawyer with the legal center that co-prosecuted Ríos Montt. Although the genocide decision was overturned, he believes that the decision is important so that events like these can never again be repeated.

General Efraín Ríos Montt

"In the panoply of commanders who turned much of Central America into a killing field in the 1980's, General Ríos Montt was one of the most murderous. He was convicted in 2013 of trying to exterminate the Ixil ethnic group, a Mayan Indian community whose villages were wiped out by his forces.

A Guatemalan judge found that the general had known about the systematic massacres in the hillside hamlets of the El Quiché department, and had done nothing to stop them or the aerial bombardment of refugees who had fled to the mountains. The conviction, seen as a landmark in human rights law, was overturned shortly afterward."

—Mario Linares

Guatemala has a long history of military coups and dictators, many of whom came from the military. The book *Bitter Fruit* is an excellent resource that tells the story of the 1950's military coup which provoked decades of conflict between the military and civilians. Unfortunately, in 2018, the conflicts continue.

These stories are about choices — those made for us by other people and those we make ourselves. The power of the Ixil womens' voices transcend the civil war. As family members and other loved ones were killed before their eyes, they had no choice but to survive.

Several decades later, when Guatemalan human rights advocates began to build the genocide case against Ríos Montt, the Ixil women chose to become plaintiffs against this powerful man. Their courage is a testament to choosing life over death.

Who Is "He"?

The Lamentation of the lxil Widows

Guatemala City, Guatemala — August 2013

In lxil
Magdalena, Ana, Maria, Juana and Cecilia
testify about thirty years ago,
the civil war.

The widows say,
"He,"
"he."
But who is "he"?

Why did he burn my house?
Why did he kill my children?
      my husband?
      my father-in-law?
      my brothers and sisters?
      my father and mother?

Why did he rape me?

Who is the man
who gave the orders?
How did he plan the attacks?

¿Quién es "él"?

La lamentación de las viudas de Ixil

Ciudad de Guatemala, Guatemala — agosto 2013

Aquí en Ixil
Las viudas Magdalena, Ana, María, Juana y Cecilia
comparten sus experiencias durante la guerra civil
hace treinta años.

"Él,"
"él,"
las viudas dicen.
¿Pero quién es "él"?

Sus preguntas en su testimonio:
¿Por qué él quemó mi casa?
¿Por qué él mató mis hijos/as,
        esposos,
        suegros/as,
        hermanos/as,
        padres y madres?

¿Por qué él me violó?

¿Quién es el hombre
que dio las órdenes?
¿Cómo él planeó los ataques?

Why did he think that we are less than he?
We are workers and farmers,
not guerrillas.

They shout, cry out and demand,
Why is he not in jail?
The sentence was given,
but he is free — living
at home with family, food
and power.

Who is he?
He has a name.
Efraín Ríos Montt,
guilty of genocide,
guilty of crimes against humanity.

And us,
we have nothing.
Where is the justice?
Tell us,
where is the justice?

¿Por qué, por qué él pensó que nosotras somos menos que él?
Somos trabajadoras y campesinas,
no guerrilleras.

Ellas gritan, lloran y preguntan,
¿Por qué él no está en el cárcel?
¡La sentencia está allá!
Pero él está libre,
en su casa con familia, comida
y poder.

¿Quién es él?
El tiene nombre.
Efraín Ríos Montt,
culpable de genocidio
y crímenes contra la humanidad.

Y nosotras, nada.

¿Dónde está la justicia?
Una grita para justicia.
Díganos, ¿dónde está la justicia?

The Day of the Dead

Día de los Muertos

October 31 to November 2, every year

A tradition that brings Latin American families and communities together, no matter where they live, is their celebration of The Day of the Dead. It's an annual holiday where people remember and honor their deceased loved ones, and when the loved ones visit in spirit form to be with their families.

When I first experienced this holiday and its rituals, I found that the *Día de los Muertos* is not a gloomy or morbid occasion like I had originally thought it might be. Instead, it is a festive and colorful celebration during which people visit cemeteries, decorate the graves of loved ones and spend time with other family members. They also make elaborately decorated altars, called *ofrendas*, in their homes to welcome the spirits.

Origins of the holiday are rooted in a combination of indigenous beliefs and the Catholic teachings the Spanish brought to Mesoamerica in the early 1500's to stamp out indigenous religious practices. Catholic teachings intermingled with the indigenous *Cosmovisións* to create new traditions. *Día de los Muertos* emerged as a combination of Catholic holidays — All Hallows' Eve, All Saints' Day and All Souls' Day — and indigenous beliefs about an afterlife in which the essence or spirits of people continue to live.

You'll see families preparing offerings of special foods and things the spirits enjoyed in life; these are laid out on the *ofrenda,* where the spirits can partake of their essence and aroma. Other items on the altar include sugar skulls, called *calaveras*; a special bread baked for the occasion (*pan de muerto*); and Aztec marigolds (*cempasúchil*), which lend a special fragrance to the altar for our departed loved ones to follow. The Day of the Dead is a celebration of the life and the relationship the family had with each person being remembered. Laying out the altar — finding photographs, searching for the right *calaveras* and preparing the departed's favorite foods and drink — lets everyone remember each person and what they mean. In celebrating who these loved ones were, we keep them all alive.

Further Resources

If you want to learn more about *Día de los Muertos*, there are two further resources I recommend: the movie *Coco* and the book *The Skeleton at the Feast.* *Coco* is a Pixar movie which explores the Day of the Dead. It has been praised for its animation, voice acting, music, emotional story, and respect for Mexican culture. *The Skeleton at the Feast: The Day of the Dead in Mexico*, is a book by Elizabeth Carmichael and Chloe Sayer. It explores both the historic origins of this holiday and its colorful present-day celebrations in Mexico and the United States.

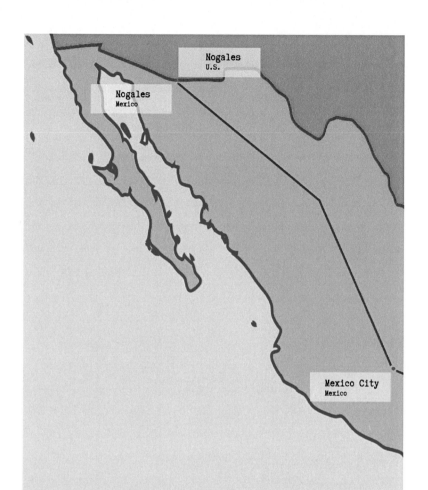

Migration
Is Not a Crime

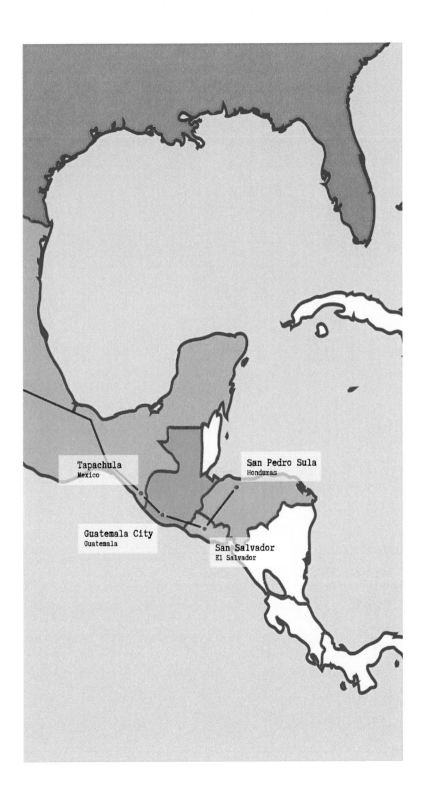

¡Bienvenida!

Welcome to America!

"Borders are set up to define the places that are safe and unsafe, to distinguish us from them. A border is a dividing line, a narrow strip along a steep edge. A borderland is a vague and undetermined place created by the emotional residue of an unnatural boundary. It is in a constant state of transition. The prohibited and forbidden are its inhabitants."

— Gloria E. Anzaldúa

Portland, Oregon — 2014

I had been on a rampage to find a way to help unaccompanied minors. I could not stand idly by when the U.S. government started housing children from Central America in large jail-like detention centers in Texas near the Mexico - U.S. Border.

I asked my friend Linda, a national church executive with the Justice and Witness Ministries, "How can I help? I speak Spanish and know why these kids are fleeing to the U.S.?"

She responded, "Pat, why don't you go to the border as a volunteer? My office can help you make the connections."

"OK." With a stipend from the church, off I went to Tucson, Arizona. A local pastor provided a room and telephone contacts with several groups which help newly arrived immigrants. Within two weeks, I was working in a shelter and learning about immigration realities at the border.

27

On one of the mornings after I had arrived, Jorge calls me. "Hi, do you have time this afternoon to help at the transition shelter for women and children immigrants, as we have a full house?"

"Sure, I will come right over."

When I arrive at the shelter, I open the door, my eyes adjusting from the blinding sunshine to the dark house. "*Hola, buenas tardes,*" I say.

"*Buenas tardes,*" respond the women seated on the living room couches, silently watching Spanish television while their small children run around.

I smell the aroma of *albóndigas* soup and sautéed *chiles*. It smells like home in Guatemala or Mexico. I feel the welcome, the *bienvenida.*

I ask the lead volunteer, a mature Mexican-American woman with a sweet smile and warm embrace, "Lorena, how many today?"

"Four women and five children," she answers. "Three women from Guatemala and one from Honduras arrived last night. We are expecting a few more later after ICE releases them to travel to their families." ICE is the acronym for U.S. Immigration and Customs Enforcement.

This shelter is already crowded — two small bedrooms with two bunk beds and a crib plus donated clothing jammed into closets. The kitchen is the center of activity as volunteers prepare huge pots of soup and the women wash dishes and feed their children.

As we chop onions, tomatoes and chilies, a volunteer asks, "Why are there such problems? My family came from Mexico fifty years ago and we didn't have any problems."

I think to myself — you are lucky, because in these times one risks one's life crossing the Sonoran desert in Arizona due to restricted entrances in border cities.

After cooking, I go outside to help with the laundry and meet a young woman from Guatemala.

"¿Cómo está?"

"Bien," she answers with a shy smile.

I ask if I can help.

While we fold clothes, her story pours out of her:

"We come from the southern coast of Guatemala, my four-year-old son and me. My husband didn't come because we had heard that women and children were more likely to be allowed to stay in the United States. *¡Mira!* I was living with my in-laws. When my father-in-law drank, he got mean and yelled and hit our son, Juanito. My son was terrified of him. Whenever my father-in-law came home drunk, I hid him in another room. Then my son stopped speaking. My husband didn't see any way to stop his father. Finally, my mother-in-law told me to go, to flee to the United States. She's the one who gave me the money for the bus fare, so we left."

She looks at me fearfully. "When I crossed into the United States near Tucson with the help of a *coyote*, I spent two nights alone in the desert with my son. We were both terrified, as we could hear the real coyotes howling nearby. Male migrants found us and threatened to harm us if we did not share our food. So I gave up our food and prayed that they would leave us alone. The Border Patrol picked us up the next day. We spent two nights at the ICE detention center and then were released to the shelter. I am going to North Carolina where I have a cousin who will help us."

She may have a good chance at asylum due to the domestic violence she was fleeing. "María, you have a lot of courage to travel a long distance to a new country where you do not speak the language."

She looks at me somewhat puzzled by the word "courage." "Paty, I just did what I had to do to protect my son. I hope that my husband can join us soon."

30

"María, look at your son — he is laughing and playing on the scooter, enjoying this beautiful sunny day. Doesn't that make you feel good?"

She gazes at me and softly tells me the cost of making the decision to leave Guatemala. "Paty, my son misses his father. It is true that he feels safe, but at night he cries and asks for his *Papi*. He would not speak in Guatemala because of his grandfather's anger and violence. I was worried about him, but now he is talking all the time. That is good."

Such bravery in the face of such daunting obstacles; I am not sure that I could make that kind of journey to save my child. But then, I don't have to make that choice, nor do most of my fellow U.S. citizens. Most of us do not understand nor live that reality.

Lorena calls out, "Pat, can you help prepare the travel bags for the families?"

We fill them with water bottles, instant soup, fresh fruit, a first-aid kit, health bars and a big, soft blanket to keep the children warm on air-conditioned buses.

"You can leave tonight," a volunteer tells the women.

They look at each other and with some nervousness reply, "*Bueno y gracias.*"

Some new women arrive. These Guatemalan women are very slender and short and probably weigh less than 100 pounds. They only speak a little Spanish. Few finish grade school because a Mayan language is their mother tongue. One woman arrives with a child wrapped only in a blanket — quickly someone takes her out to the storage area to pick out clothes for her child.

Another woman is very pregnant and walks with a cane. I help her sit down on a chair and ask her if she would like some food.

"Yes, please, but I can't walk to the table."

"No problem, I'll bring you some food, Catarina."

After she eats I ask, "*¿Qué pasa?* What is wrong with your leg?"

She grimaces and says, "I fell from the wall at the border."

"What? The fence is twenty-one feet high! How did this happen?"

"The people who were helping me made a makeshift sling to pull me up and over the fence. When I cleared the top, the sling gave way."

"Are you in pain? What happened when the Border Patrol picked you up?"

"They gave me some pain medication and wrapped my leg and told me that it probably was a sprain."

"Catarina, where are you from in Guatemala?"

"San Marcos," she replies.

"*¿Tacaná?*" I ask.

She looks surprised.

"I visited there many years ago."

Her eyes light up as she tells me about her town and family. Like many of the women she has a story of leaving a child behind. Tears form in her eyes. I close my eyes and think how tragic to have to make that kind of decision. She left due to poverty, lack of work and the hope of finding work in the United States. Her unemployed husband left her after her second pregnancy.

I ask the resident coordinator, "What will happen to her?"

He explains that she has a medical appointment that evening to see if she can travel by bus.

"But how can she travel? She has to keep her foot elevated plus the fact she is pregnant. There is no way that she can travel on a crowded bus!"

"Pat," Jorge says, "You know that we cannot keep her here and we have a full house tonight and probably more over the weekend."

I return to the living room and sit down next to Catarina. "I know this is difficult. You are very brave to have traveled so far."

She sighs and says, "I had no choice as I want my child to have a better life."

It is time for me to leave. Such mixed feelings — sad, and a bit pissed off as well as conflicted. Part of me feels at home with the Guatemalan women; it brings back both warm and painful memories of my life in Guatemala. I am concerned about the future of these women. With limited education and no English, some of them will work plucking chickens in factories or cleaning houses in order to survive.

33

ICE gives them a six-month reprieve following their initial detention before their next court hearing, with probable deportation if they do not have a good attorney. They are heading by Greyhound to reunite with a family member. I don't know what will happen to them in their new homes, but they are strong and determined. Their new communities will support them.

Acompañamiento

A Guatemalan *Amiga*

Acompañamiento is a powerful concept in Latin America. Accompaniment in one sense is an easy term. You walk with others by invitation — not behind or in front of them — lending solidarity, a shoulder, a sounding board, a word of counsel or caution. Empowering not enabling.

But in another sense, accompaniment is incredibly difficult. You must walk with people as they suffer from the violence of poverty, racism, illiteracy, social isolation and injustice. These are things that neither you nor they can fix, yet you have to manage this reality with them.

I first learned about accompaniment during the 1980's when the United States government funded the *contras,* a group of Nicaraguans in opposition to the *Sandinista* government. The *Sandinistas,* in the 1979 revolution, overthrew the government of U.S.-backed dictator, Anastasio Somoza Debayle. In July 1983, over one hundred U.S. citizens traveled to the Honduras - Nicaragua border to form a human shield to protect Nicaraguan civilians from *contra* attacks. Witness for Peace was founded from that action. Since that time, this group, along with other non-governmental organizations, have provided "witnesses" who observe, stand with and accompany people whose lives are threatened. I became an accompanier in 1993 when I was asked by Witness for Peace to watch the return of Guatemalans — who had been living in exile in Mexico — to their homes in Guatemala. Along with Peace Brigades International, we provided an international presence and "eyes" to ensure the safe return of Guatemalan families to their lands after ten years of exile in refugee camps in Mexico.

Lake Atitlán, Guatemala — 2014

The mist rises slowly off the deep blue iridescent lake. I'm sitting at my makeshift desk in a hillside *casita* looking at the three volcanoes — San Pedro, Toliman and Atitlán — that loom over this beautiful lake in the central highlands of Guatemala. It is paradise in the midst of a troubled country. In the winter of 2014, I came to reconnect with the part of my heart that lives in Guatemala and to share stories from my lifelong love affair with its people and their country.

I travel north to Quetzaltenango, the second largest city in Guatemala. My friend Irma's niece, a teacher, tells me how drug gangs control the schools. The gangs recruit students with promises of making easy money, but the initiation rituals are brutal. Young women are gang-raped and young men are ordered to murder someone; that is how they become gang members.

"Paty, the going price on the street to murder someone is $50."

I ask, "What are parents doing to keep their children safe?"

They shake their heads, "Sadly, they see their only choice is to head north or send their children to the United States."

In the summer of 2014 thousands of children and young adults from Central America stream across the Mexico - U.S. border seeking safety and asylum. The U.S. government locks them up in windowless centers and deports many back to the violent countries they have just fled.

Tucson, Arizona — 2015

By November 2015 I am volunteering to help with newly arrived immigrant families. As a visitor to the Eloy Detention Center, a privately owned and operated prison in the middle of a desolate desert, I meet

María Luisa for the first time.

She is dressed in the yellow jumpsuit like other detainees. She bounds towards me, hugs and kisses me.

"Hola, I am María Luisa."

She is young, vivacious, with sparkling eyes and a ready smile. I am taken aback and surprised by her energy. Many other detainees are somber, crying and angry. She immediately tells me her story, an all too familiar tale for young women who attempt to travel through Mexico on their own to the United States.

"I'm from the northern part of Guatemala near the Mexico border. My partner was involved with drugs and abused me. My *Papi* needs kidney dialysis and must travel three times a week to Quetzaltenango for treatment which is expensive. I decided to flee my abusive partner and to head north to earn money to help my father."

She was kidnapped by a Mexican drug cartel, held hostage and sexually abused until a cousin in Florida paid $8,000 to ransom her. It is common practice for drug cartels to seize cell phones and then call family members to extort money for their captured family members. When María Luisa crossed the U.S. border, she was apprehended and sent to the Eloy Detention Center. Her crime was entry into the United States.

A few tears appeared in her eyes as she describes the daily humiliations by detention center staff as well as the horrible food, a common complaint among detainees. Her spirit and determination to be released move me. Despite her situation, she laughs a lot and befriends other detainees. She believes that God is watching over her and that her prayers are what sustain her.

I visit her several times before my return to Portland. I do not see her for another year but we write frequently. I send a letter of support for her bond hearing. She excitedly tells me that she has found a *pro bono* attorney with the help of the visitation program and will have representation at her court hearings. Her bail is finally set at $20,000. *My God, I could not raise that amount.* Her aunt in Colorado sold a car and some property and was able to raise $5,000, and her attorneys paid the remaining $15,000, an unusual act.

In January 2017, I return to the Eloy Detention Center.

María Luisa is elated. "Paty, I'm going to get out."

She is released in late January to a halfway house in Tucson. The first night she puts on makeup for the first time in fifteen months, dances happily with the other young women living in the house and eats lots of beans, rice and tortillas.

"I'm free, Paty, thanks to you and the other volunteers who befriended me."

The next day I put her on a bus to Colorado where she will live with her aunt and work in a potato factory once her visa is approved.

With hugs and tears we say goodbye. "Let's stay in touch." She smiles and waves as she boards the bus.

Then, silence. I send a few cards and leave messages for her aunt. A Tucson friend hears from her Guatemalan family that she is okay and has a Facebook page. I send her a friend request and we are eventually able to reconnect.

"I'm in L.A. now, Paty. I am working for a family."

She has a lot of questions about her immigration status and asks if I can call her lawyer in Arizona. He assures me that her case is closed and she has a T (Trafficking) visa with employment authorization for four years.

I call her with the good news but I am still worried about her. "Are you okay, María Luisa? Does the family treat you well? Where do you live?"

She doesn't respond to my barrage of questions but says that she will see me soon when I am in Los Angeles.

In mid-January we have a joyous reunion on my sister's patio — hugs, kisses, laughter — a new boyfriend from El Salvador drove her here! She is beaming. Life is good.

"Paty, I left Colorado because I couldn't earn enough money to repay the $8,000 ransom plus the $5,000 my aunt raised for the bond."

I assure her that the U.S. government will refund her aunt and the attorneys for the bond.

"Also, I was lonely in the small town in Colorado. Besides my family and taking care of their children, there was nothing to do."

The good news is that her work family wants to help her learn English. She is a high-school graduate and is bright, so she should learn English easily. We talked about how soon she can become a permanent resident and, ultimately, a United States citizen.

The only moment of tears was when she shared that her beloved *Papi* had died five months earlier. "I only came north to help my *Papi* get better." She has paid a high price personally to be in the United States.

But then, being María Luisa, she tells me of her hopes of bringing her mother to live with her in Los Angeles, at least for a visit. Her story does have a happy ending after a great deal of pain and struggle. She is a beautiful young woman and a determined one. Her Facebook posts are enthusiastic and full of prayers of gratitude.

As she and her boyfriend depart, she gives me numerous hugs and kisses. She smiles and asks me, "Would you like to be a grandmother for the child I want to have?"

"Yes, María Luisa, but not now. Take your time and enjoy your new life."

They leave in time to go to the beach, to see the Pacific Ocean and to walk the boardwalk. Later, she sends an effusive Facebook post, ending as her letters always did: *¡Dios y los angelitos los cuiden!* May God and the angels take care of you!

Portland, Oregon — 2018

Almost fifty years ago, I went to Guatemala with my husband Carlo. We had never worked in a "developing country" and had no knowledge of Guatemala's culture and history or the role of the U.S. interventions into its politics. The rural highland village where we lived warmly welcomed us. Our Spanish was hard to understand. Although I did not know how to cook, I taught cooking classes and Carlo experimented with new crops with the farmers. People hugged us, invited us into their homes, walked with us to appointments so that we couldn't get lost and accepted us into their community. We became friends.

How could I not do the same for newcomers to our country? I know the Central American realities and why people migrate north seeking safety and a chance to earn a living wage. I want to welcome them as they welcomed me.

My other reason for accompanying the newly arrived immigrants is to engage in resistance. Accompanying people helps them avoid deportation and detention. I believe in a United States that welcomes immigrants, like those who helped to build this country. Our democratic values are still a beacon of light to many people. I work to ensure that this beacon of light continues.

Becoming an UndocuAngel!

As an immigration attorney in Tucson, Arizona, Mo Goldman coined the phrase UndocuAngels and initiated a program to link undocumented immigrants to U.S. citizens. *The Daily Wildcat* — the Arizona State University newspaper — has an excellent article from February 2017 about this program and its "efforts to offer a strong sense of protection to the immigrant community in Tucson."

Goldman says it well, "If a person were to get arrested and they need access to legal documents, or if they get taken into detention and they need legal help getting released, maybe that U.S. citizen would be able to help them." Many times these are our neighbors — who are suddenly in legal trouble, separated from their families and so on. The only thing that has changed for many of these immigrants is the legal environment, and we can move forward to support them.

Tucson, Arizona — 2017

"I'm so excited about seeing my father after eighteen years," a vibrant woman with dark hair tells me over a cup of coffee.

We are sitting in the basement of a United Methodist church that has opened its doors to shelter women and men traveling with young children. It is a large room with mattresses on the floor and suitcases and clothing scattered around. Graciela is from El Salvador and is with her four-year-old daughter, who shares a shy smile from her mother's side. This little girl has the same dark, beautiful eyes as her mother.

"We had to leave El Salvador. The gangs demanded that I pay half of my rent to them. I couldn't afford that. It wasn't safe so I left my

43

husband to travel north to reunite with my father in New England. My father has worked in a hotel for twenty years and he has a job for me. I am going to work hard for him and my daughter."

What will Graciela find in cold New England? Like most immigrants, she is prepared to work hard, enroll her daughter in school and study English. She is definitely motivated. Will she be safe? Before leaving the shelter, each person receives information that advises them to show up for their court date and how to avoid deportation. ICE gives each parent and child six months to apply for asylum or to get an attorney in order to remain in the U.S. But now the new ICE priority is to deport immigrants who've been in the United States for less than two years.

Another person in the shelter is Juan, a short, sturdy man with Mayan features. Juan is traveling with his five-year-old son who loves to play soccer. He and another boy kick a big ball in the empty basement space, laughing and shouting, "Goal!"

Juan continues, "There is no work in my rural northern town of Guatemala. I have to support my family — the most that I could earn was $5 a day. My mother is a legal permanent resident." He tells me proudly, "My mother is a pastor of a Pentecostal church in the Southeast. She urged me to come north to join her. I need to work. What kind of job do you think that I can find? Because, as soon as possible, we will bring the rest of our family."

Juan is determined to build a better life. He has hope that he can do that in the U.S. I don't tell him that most of the jobs will be low-paying but what do I know? He may find a way to save money and send for his family.

At Casa Alitas, another shelter in a nondescript house, I talk with Juana, a young indigenous woman from Guatemala.

Juana speaks quietly, "I am going to meet my sister in the Middle West. In my poor rural village I was living with my mother-in-law and two daughters. My husband is in the United States but he has found another woman."

She leans towards me, "I am nervous about the bus trip because we will have to change buses in Dallas, Texas. I don't read or write but I know that my older daughter will help me.

I look at the seven- and eight-year-old daughters playing next to us with wide smiles.

Confidently, she says "My daughters will learn quickly and have a better life in the U.S. and I am getting on the bus!"

Later, she shows me how to make Guatemalan rice — I chop tomatoes, onions and garlic.

Her face lights up and she laughs, "I love to cook and did all the cooking for my mother-in-law and children." She, like the other recent arrivals, committed an illegal act by crossing the border — the first time is a misdemeanor. If she is deported and crosses again, it is a felony and she will serve time in a federal detention center.

I sense her strength to have traveled from Guatemala to the United States alone with her two beautiful daughters. I am hopeful that her sister will support her, but she may not qualify for political asylum, as the federal government will say that she is an economic migrant. Will her six-month humanitarian parole paper from ICE protect her from the increasing ICE raids?

Guatemalan indigenous women are the poorest people in Guatemala. They suffer from the triple oppressions of being a woman, being indigenous and being poor. Most of the indigenous women I met in the shelter came from the three poorest states in the northern highlands of Guatemala.

During the 1980's civil war, many of them — like the Ixil women who testified against Ríos Montt — were killed, raped or tortured. It is no surprise that many have chosen to travel north despite the obstacles of gangs and police demanding bribes, of kidnapping for ransom and of sexual violence by the Mexican police and cartels alike.

Prior to Trump's presidency in 2017, the "catch and release" procedure allowed families with children and asylum seekers to be released on their own recognizance to wait for their immigration hearing. The Bush administration had begun this practice due to the overcrowding of detention centers, and the Obama administration continued it.

Tucson ICE offices had followed this practice, releasing families to nonprofit shelters and, ultimately, to their families elsewhere in the United States. The "catch and release" for families traveling with children was only used within a hundred miles of the border. Under the Trump administration, now ICE can detain any undocumented immigrant anywhere in the U.S. without a hearing before a judge. Inwardly, I scream: *Is the United States a democracy or a police state?*

In addition to working with recently arrived immigrants in Tucson, I travel across the border from Nogales, Arizona to visit *El Comedor*, a cafeteria that serves food to those who have been recently deported and strives to maintain their human dignity in the midst of a dehumanizing process. While I'm there, I sit next to a woman from the Mexican state of Chiapas. Her name is María; she has just been deported.

María notices a well-dressed woman crying while surrounded by tall men in suits. "Who is she?" María asks in a whisper.

"I don't know," I reply, "but all the Mexican officials mean that something big has happened to her."

The woman is Guadalupe García de Rayos, the first person deported from Phoenix under Trump's new overarching immigration policies. The press with cameras appears to ask Guadalupe about what happened when she was detained. Guadalupe has two U.S.-born children and has reported regularly to the local ICE office where she was recently detained and deported. She is staying in Nogales, Mexico at a safe place to be near her family.

Under the Obama administration she would not have been a deportation priority. That administration prioritized deporting people with serious criminal records, not families. Now it seems the rules have changed. The raids against undocumented immigrants have begun and I fear that many families will be separated. Everyone who overstays a visa or who crosses the border without official permission can now be deported.

Portland, Oregon — 2017

When I returned to Portland in the winter of 2017, I heard about a local example of being an UndocuAngel. Latino parishioners were being harassed as they entered their Roman Catholic church in Southeast Portland. What happened? Word went out and the next Sunday, 200 UndocuAngels surrounded the church to protect the documented and undocumented parishioners. The angels sent a strong message: *We will not tolerate racist abuse and intimidation!*

Many of the women did not tell me their stories of experiencing violence in their home countries or on the journey north. If they seek asylum, then they will tell the entire story to an attorney. However, I know the statistics on femicide in Guatemala as well as the numbers of women who have been raped or kidnapped in Mexico. They deserve a fair hearing for asylum in the United States. Hopefully there will be U.S. citizens ready to help them in the communities where they finally reside.

Crossing Borders

Migration or Immigration?

"You cannot live in hope, or look to the future if you do not first know how to value yourselves [...] your life, your hands, your history, is worth the effort."

—Pope Francis, Mexico, 2016

As a U.S. citizen and a white middle-class woman, I have had the privilege of crossing many borders. I have never been stopped by a customs official nor detained in a government-operated center. I have traveled to the Middle East, Africa, Europe, Latin America and the Caribbean. My U.S. passport has opened the door for me. I am very aware of my travel privilege.

What is the difference between migration and immigration? People migrate to another country. Migration is not recognized as an international human right by the United Nations, although the U.N. High Commissioner on Human Rights and Pope Francis call for respect of migrants' human rights as they move from one country to another.

Sovereign nations have the right to establish immigration policies and to define criteria for entry into their country. With more than 258 million people migrating today, migration and immigration have become more challenging for those who wish to leave their home, as well as the sending and receiving countries.

In 1965, the United States passed the Immigration and Naturalization Act which replaced the racially based quotas with preferential categories based on family relationships and job skills —

giving particular preference to potential immigrants with relatives in the United States and with occupations deemed critical by the U.S. Department of Labor.

Subsequent Congressional legislation granted amnesty to approximately three million immigrants in 1986. There have been attempts to fix the "broken" immigration systems by members of both political parties, but no compromise has succeeded in changing the existing laws.

Santa María Tzejá, Guatemala — 2016

After five months in Arizona listening to the stories of the women's journeys and the causes for their migration north, I have the opportunity to visit a Guatemalan rural community in the Ixcán that has invested in educating its youth. I want their perspective on migration.

I greet Juana, my friend and the social studies teacher. "*Hola, Juana.*" She smiles and presents me to her class.

Juana has asked me to talk about immigration to the U.S. "Please welcome a visitor, Patricia, who has worked with migrants in the United States. Please give her your attention."

It is a hot, humid afternoon. The classroom is in an old wood building and has one fan that slowly circulates warm air. It is the last class of the day and the students are tired. They are twelve- and thirteen-year-olds — eighth-graders — and there are about fifteen of them gazing at me. It is awkward at first. I ask if someone can draw a map of Guatemala, Mexico and the U.S. on the whiteboard — to show the borders and outlines of the three countries. One boy volunteers but then shakes his head no. I quickly draw a rough outline emphasizing the borders that separate the three countries.

The point of the map is to understand *fronteras* (borders). "Did you know that there was no border between Chiapas, Mexico and Guatemala until the late 1800's? Mayan people could move freely north and south. Then a border was drawn to divide Mexico from Guatemala." I continue, "And Mexico used to extend up the west coast to the state of Oregon and included much of the southwest region of the United States until the Mexican-American War. Borders were again redrawn."

I try a joke. "A Mexican-American friend of mine told me, 'Pat, I did not cross the border, the border crossed me.'" Some smiles appear on a few faces. I want to involve them in this discussion so I ask, "How many of you have family members in the United States?" Hands shoot up. "Who are they? Where do they live and what do they do?"

About a third of the class has family living in the North. A young woman — maybe thirteen years old, sitting in the back row — says quietly, "*Mi madre.*"

Oh, my God, it is so painful to hear that. I blurt out, "How sad!" and ask, "Where does your mother live?" She shakes her head slowly. She looks down at the floor and I feel helpless. I want to do something for her but in reality, I can't. Only one of the nine students knows where his family member lives and what he does for a living.

"Why do people migrate?" I ask.

A small boy with laughing eyes holds up his hand with the universal gesture meaning money. There is a murmur of assent around the room. Behind this answer are the questions: Why do we have to migrate to find work? Why are there no jobs in Guatemala that can support a family?

Juana reminds the restless kids to pay attention. I can understand why they'd like to be outside playing at the end of the day rather than wrestling with the heavy topic of immigration. I share my work on the Mexico - U.S. border and the challenges migrants face upon entering the U.S. Then, I divide the students into small groups and ask them to develop one question they want to ask this visitor from the North.

Their questions range from innocent ones — Why are there borders? — to more painful ones — Why doesn't the U.S. president like migrants? One boy asks, "Why do Americans hate us?"

I stammer a bit as I say, "Well, the drug gangs that plague your country, Honduras and El Salvador, are not only scary to you but also to people in the United States. The president tries to paint all immigrants as criminals. He also says that immigrants are coming to take people's jobs.

In reality the jobs that most immigrants do, many North Americans will not do. Since most migrants don't speak English, some states have tried to pass laws that require everyone to speak English."

I try to answer all their questions honestly, but it is difficult to justify what many regard as an unfair immigration policy and politicians who stir up racist fears about migrants taking jobs. The U.S. political system is filled with complexities, but these children certainly know that they are not wanted.

In the village, life will be pretty bleak for the graduates who can't continue their education. They'll earn about $30 a month if they work on their family farm after completing middle school. This is a good middle school where students study current affairs and learn English as well as Spanish and K'iche', their Mayan language. Most of them want to continue their education, but that takes money and there is no high school nearby. There are some scholarships, but not all families can afford the costs of room and board. If there are neither jobs nor educational opportunities at home, then the dangers of the trip north do not appear so difficult to these twelve- to thirteen-year-olds who want a better life.

This village is deeply committed to its community and the villagers resolve conflicts communally. Unlike students in many Guatemalan public schools, students here learn about the thirty-six year civil war and the genocide that continued into the early 1990's.

Santiago, a village leader, is very worried about the youth leaving. Although their grandparents suffered through the 1982 massacre and the flight to Mexico, the grandchildren did not. They do know family members who suffered greatly during the thirty-six year internal armed conflict and are taught to respect their Mayan language and culture. Is this enough to interest students to stay and build a strong community?

The village commemorates the massacre annually and the youth have produced a play about that event. Two village elders who survived the massacre speak at a middle-school assembly about the importance of community in their survival.

Students have access to the internet at the school's computer center. They may not have running water in the village, but they do have electricity, television, cell phones and access to Facebook. Santiago asks, "What will happen to them? What can we do to instill the communal values in their lives? They place more emphasis on the individual than the community."

He adds, "I thought at one time, I would have to leave and go north. Fortunately, I found a way to support my passion for telling our stories through our local television programs. Other young adults my age who grew up in Mexico in refugee camps are staying in the area after finishing the university in order to strengthen our community. We need to find ways to keep our children in Guatemala."

I am moved by his honesty about the challenges to a village that has invested so much in its youth. It is true that these students, unlike others in public schools in Guatemala City, do learn about the genocide and know family members who fled after the 1982 massacre. But the young people now face another reality in Guatemala — a country that does not invest in education, health care or economic infrastructure, especially for its Mayan indigenous population. The drug gangs and wars are dangerous and the Guatemalan military does not stop the gangs. In fact, some military officers have been prosecuted because of their links to organized crime. This village, like many others in Central America, faces tremendous external challenges in keeping its families intact.

Are there alternatives and incentives for young Guatemalans not to migrate but to develop a strong future at home? At a forum for youth

54

in Cantabal, I heard a litany of human rights challenges in Guatemala. A local indigenous leader denounced a list of multinational mega-projects that do not benefit the community. All the speakers attacked the Alliance for Prosperity, the plan proposed by the Obama administration in 2015 to help the governments of Honduras, El Salvador and Guatemala. Its stated purpose is to stop migration and to strengthen economic development, but as one speaker observed: "It is an industrial development approach. Multinationals will build factories from Chiquimula to Zacapa, from the western to eastern regions of Guatemala. Who benefits? Certainly not the local Guatemalans who will work for low wages."

A Mexican migration activist at this regional assembly talked about free-trade agreements that have displaced small farmers and created low-paying jobs in factories instead. The students already know about a multinational company's plans to build a large dam on the nearby Chixoy River that would displace more farmers by flooding their farmlands.

The speakers challenged the students to get involved. The students were asked when they returned to their schools to select a project to work on — to get involved in determining their future. The underlying causes of migration are big ones for ninth-graders to tackle — no health care, employment, respect for human rights and omnipresent violence. What project would the students decide to do?

It felt surreal. In the United States, our government thinks that migrants are the problem. But in Guatemala, the United States is perceived to be the problem because of our government's actions during the 1980's and into the present. Guatemalans know that the U.S. government — under President Reagan in the 1980's — supplied arms and training to the dictator Efraín Ríos Montt. The resulting civil war killed approximately two hundred thousand civilians, and more than two million Guatemalans were displaced. The first wave of migration from Guatemala into the United States was in the early 1980's as people fled the violence of the war and sought sanctuary in the U.S.

Now, the United States government pays Mexico millions of dollars to militarize the Guatemala - Mexico border in order to stop migrants there. Despite the barriers, thirty thousand Guatemalans immigrate annually to the United States.

The view from the South is different from that in the North. Guatemalans fear the loss of an entire generation to migration. They are trying to educate, motivate and challenge youth to take responsibility for the future of their country. In the United States we do not want more immigrants from Guatemala, Honduras and El Salvador, yet the United States has been deeply involved in the destabilization of these three countries for many decades. My own journey to Guatemala began in 1969 where I learned about Colonel Carlos Manuel Arana Osorio, a right-wing military officer referred to as the "Butcher of Zacapa." In 1966 he began a military campaign — with guidance and training from the U.S. army's Green Berets — against small farmers, resulting in several thousand deaths. The farmers wanted land reform and access to titles of the land they were working. It was an eye-opening experience and one that led me on my activist journey.

Accompaniment Continues

Portland, Oregon — 2018

In the sixteen months since my time at the Arizona - Mexico border, the on-the-ground reality has changed considerably. The new zero-tolerance policy has created a very different reality for immigrants as well as the humanitarian organizations working to assist them. Back in Portland, I have dedicated this past year to "accompanying" undocumented persons to ICE check-ins, ICE court hearings and misdemeanor and felony hearings in local courts. The Interfaith Movement for Immigrant Justice, working with ACLU legal observers, has trained over forty people to do accompaniment work. Most recently, we have received an asylum applicant and child from Honduras.

There is a lot to do wherever you live in the United States. As U.S. citizens, each of us can let an immigrant neighbor know that we are ready to protect them if ICE shows up at their door. If each of us takes a *Know Your Rights* workshop — in order to understand our basic rights and those of undocumented persons — and gets to know our neighbors, we can know where, when and how we're needed. One way to make ourselves available is to volunteer to teach or tutor English through a local nonprofit agency, school or community college.

The policy changes that the Trump administration has initiated — including, most recently, family separation — are devastating, not just to immigrant families, but also to our standing as a democracy that welcomes immigrants and respects their human rights.

As a Tucson friend said, "Pat, everyone who comes through the shelters here is going someplace else in the United States." This is a call to get involved in your local community. After all, most of our family stories are immigrant stories.

Here are three opportunities:

Freedom for Immigrants - I visited the Eloy Detention Center through this program. There are over forty visitation programs in the United States operated through this organization.

https://www.freedomforimmigrants.org/

Sanctuary Movement - For people of faith and conscience, look for the Sanctuary Movement in your community or state.

https://www.sanctuarynotdeportation.org/

Immigrant Rights Coalitions - The American Friends Service Committee supports immigrant rights programs in the United States.

https://www.afsc.org/sanctuaryeverywhere

This is the time for every U.S citizen to take action, get involved and be prepared to have your life transformed. Mine has. The journey of accompaniment — beginning in Guatemala in 1969 — changed my life. I have spent the past forty-nine years involved in justice work in Latin America and the United States.

Several years ago, in a senior Capstone class at Portland State University, we were discussing the imbalance of power between "developed" countries in the Global North and "developing" countries in the Global South.

A student asked me, "Why are you an activist, Professor Rumer? You sound like a 60's radical!"

"Yes, damn right and proud of it!" I responded.

He paused and then quietly asked, "How did you become an activist? And how do you sustain yourself in the struggle for justice?"

I laughed and replied, "It would take a long time — in fact, a lifetime — to share the experiences that created the activist that you see today." But perhaps, part of the answer lies in these stories.

In another Capstone course working with the Latina community, a student asked, "Why do you care?"

Whenever we open our hearts and heads to listen to others' experiences, the chances are that we will encounter new truths and realities that challenge us. In the 1960's, U.S. Senator Robert Kennedy toured the American South to learn about poverty. He came from a privileged, wealthy family in the Northeast and this tour changed his life as he saw U.S. citizens living in conditions that were unimaginable to him. It transformed his views on poverty, and led him to run for U.S. president on a pledge to address the root causes of poverty.

I invite all readers to break your heart wide open and to listen and accompany newcomers to our society.

Patricia J. Kumer

Bio

Lifetime activist and educator Patricia Rumer fell in love with Guatemala in 1969 as a community development volunteer with the American Friends Service Committee working in a rural highland, K'iche'-speaking community. She has returned frequently to unite with the part of her heart that will always live there.

Throughout a prolific forty-five years of activism, educational and international leadership, Rumer has traveled extensively in Latin America, the Caribbean, the Middle East and Africa. Patricia was strongly influenced by her early Guatemalan experiences working with Paolo Friere's popular education literacy program as well as with Roman Catholic nuns and priests who preached and lived a liberating Gospel. She saw the impact of Liberation Theology in organizing poor communities to become involved in social justice struggles and saw them become leaders in their own communities. She believes in a radical, inclusive spiritual practice and has worked to incorporate those early experiences into her life work.

As a Witness for Peace observer she accompanied Guatemalan refugees displaced by the 1980's internal armed conflict in their return from Mexico to Guatemala (1993,1995) and their resettlement in the Ixcan. In 2013 after the Ríos Montt genocide trial she was a member of the Guatemalan Human Rights Commission/USA delegation to investigate the impact of the genocide decision on Guatemalan human rights defenders. In 2016 she witnessed the Sepur Zarco trial in which a Guatemalan judge convicted two former military officers of crimes against humanity on counts of rape, murder and slavery from 1982-88.

Patricia has a PhD in Urban and Public Affairs from Portland State University. From 2008-15 she taught senior international Capstone courses that focused on women and indigenous communities in community development. She also organized two student-immersion courses to Chiapas, Mexico.

Since her retirement from teaching, she has been working on a book that describes her own transformational life journey along with those Central American human rights workers with whom she has shared their struggles for justice. Recently she worked with Central American immigrants in Tucson, Arizona. Her writings on Central America and immigration-related stories have appeared in *Streetroots*, *Common Lot*, at Los Porteños events and in her blog, www.justiceactivist.com.

Further Resources on Guatemala

Bitter Fruit:
The Story of the American Coup in Guatemala
A comprehensive account of the CIA operation to overthrow the democratically-elected government of Jacobo Arbenz of Guatemala in 1954. Written by Stephen Schlesinger and Stephen Kinzer and published by the Inter-American Development Bank in 2005.

Efraín Ríos Montt,
Guatemalan Dictator Convicted of Genocide, Dies at 91
This article describes the dictator's past actions and clarifies why he was convicted of genocide charges. Written by Mario Linares and published on April 1, 2018 in *The New York Times*.
https://www.nytimes.com/2018/04/01/obituaries/efrain-rios-montt-guatemala-dead.html

Guatemala Human Rights Commission
A humanitarian organization that monitors the human rights situation in Guatemala.
http://www.ghrc-usa.org/

The Guatemala Reader
In choosing the selections for this anthology, the editors sought to avoid representing the country only in terms of its long experience of conflict, racism, and violence. It portrays Guatemala as a real place where people experience real joys. The editors introduce the selections in relation to neoliberalism, multiculturalism, and the dynamics of migration to the U.S. Written by Greg Grandin, Deborah T. Levenson, and Elizabeth Oglesby and published by Duke University Press in 2011.

Granito:
How to Nail a Dictator
A film about the ways *When the Mountains Tremble*, provided key evidence for bringing the genocide indictment against Efraín Ríos Montt. It shows the burgeoning generation of human rights activists that grew up in the wake of Ríos Montt's crimes. Produced by Skylight Pictures in 2012.

Guatemala's Genocide on Trial

The courts vacated Efraín Ríos Montt's conviction, but the struggle for justice continues. This article remembers the survivors' courage. Written by Kate Doyle and published on May 22, 2013 in *The Nation*. https://www.thenation.com/article/guatemalas-genocide-trial/

I, Rigoberta Menchú:
An Indian Woman in Guatemala

In this book, Rigoberta Menchú, a Guatemalan peasant woman, reflects on the experiences common to many Indian communities in Latin America. Written by Rigoberta Menchú, Elisabeth Burgos-Debray and Ann Wright and published by Verso in 2010.

Paradise in Ashes:
A Guatemalan Journey of Courage, Terror, and Hope

An account of the violence and repression that defined the Guatemalan civil war. The books tells the story of the village of Santa María Tzejá and why it embodies the forces and conflicts that define the country today. Written by Beatriz Manz and Aryeh Neier and published by the University of California Press in 2005.

Return of Guatemala's Refugees:
Reweaving the Torn

On February 13, 1982, the Guatemalan army stormed into the remote northern Guatemala village of Santa María Tzejá. This book describes the experiences of the survivors who stayed behind and those who fled to Mexico where they learned to organize and defend their rights. Written by Clark Taylor and published by Temple University Press in 1998.

Seeds of Freedom:
Liberating Education in Guatemala

This book begins in the 70's, when the majority of the villagers from Santa María Tzejá were illiterate farmers working in conditions close to slavery. By 2010, nearly all the village children are educated, frequently to a university level. Santa María Tzejá has come to exemplify the theory and practice of liberating education and the radical pedagogy of Paulo Freire. Written by Clark Taylor and published by Paradigm in 2013.

When the Mountains Tremble

A film about the struggle of Guatemala's Mayan population against a heritage of state and foreign oppression. It is centered on the experiences of Rigoberta Menchú. Produced by Skylight Pictures in 1983.

Further Resources on Immigration

Acting for Immigration Justice/Luchadora por la justicia
Pat Rumer's website and blog.
https://www.justiceactivist.com/

American Friends Service Committee
An organization that promotes lasting peace with justice, as a practical expression of faith in action.
https://www.afsc.org/

Borderlands/La Frontera:
The New Mestiza
The essays and poems in this volume remap our understanding of what a *border* is. It is not a simple divide between here and there, us and them, but a psychic, social and cultural terrain that we inhabit. Written by Gloria E. Anzaldúa and published by Aunt Lute Books in 1987.

Border Patrol Nation:
Dispatches from the Front Lines of Homeland Security
This book sounds the alarm as it combines first-hand encounters with careful research to expose a vast and booming industry for high-end technology, weapons, surveillance, and prisons. While politicians and corporations reap substantial profits, the experiences of millions of men, women, and children point to staggering humanitarian consequences. A book by Todd Miller; published by City Lights in 2014.

Detained and Deported:
Stories of Immigrant Families Under Fire
Inside the massive Eloy Detention Center, in a Nogales soup kitchen and elsewhere, this book shows how detention and deportation policies have broadened police powers, while enriching a private prison industry. It also documents the rise of resistance, profiling activists who are fighting for the rights of the undocumented. Written by Margaret Regan and published by Beacon Press in 2015.

Enrique's Journey:
The Story of a Boy's Dangerous Odyssey to Reunite with His Mother
A book that puts a human face on the ongoing debate about immigration reform in the United States. It recounts the quest of a Honduran boy looking for his mother, eleven years after she is forced to leave her starving family to find work in the United States. Written by Pulitzer Prize winner Sonia Nazario and published by Random House in 2007.

Freedom for Immigrants
An organization that is devoted to abolishing immigration detention and ending the isolation of those currently suffering in the system.
https://www.freedomforimmigrants.org/

Guatemala - U.S. Migration:
Transforming Regions
This book analyzes migration to the U.S. in a regional context including Guatemala, Mexico and the United States. Seamlessly blending multiple sociological perspectives, it incorporates gendered as well as ethnic and class dimensions of migration. Written by Susanne Jonas and Néstor Rodriguez and published by the University of Texas Press in 2014.

Pedagogy of the Oppressed
The methodology of Paulo Freire has empowered many impoverished and illiterate people throughout the world. Freire's work has taken on special urgency in the U.S. and Western Europe, where the creation of a permanent underclass among the underprivileged and minorities in cities and urban centers is increasingly accepted as the norm. Written by Paulo Friere and published by Herder and Herder in 1970.

Storming the Wall:
Climate Change, Migration, and Homeland Security
This book chronicles a growing system of militarized divisions between the rich and the poor, the environmentally secure and the environmentally exposed. Stories of crisis, greed and violence are juxtaposed with powerful examples of solidarity and hope. Written by Todd Miller and published by City Lights in 2017.

Made in the USA
San Bernardino, CA
02 April 2019